Another
cre(*crust*)ation
by

Sponsored by...

THE MEGA OVEN

industrial strength and Zap Nugget ready.

The Opti-Plex 380 by Dell offers a rigorous, all enclosed reinforced plastic hard shell with all the trimmings. if you're one of those "computer freaks" that wants to know a bunch of specific bull crap about it, than you're missing the point & you probably can't handle this kind of machine anyways.

It's 380.
it's Opti-Plex Ready.
It's Dell.
Deal with it.

I'll Sell You One of My Scabs for a Dollar
(The Story of Lickory Lee)

One day I was sitting in my room watching a TV that I had bought with my money
I had other things I had bought as well, a card game, a rolodex, and a machine that sucks the fat out of your tummy
Was this enough for me, not in the least
I wanted more, I wanted everything,I wanted to be the king of the feast
Perhaps a little plan is what my life needs
A plan so pompous it will be laced with my greed
I will go in to business and squander a profit
I'll have so much money I'll put new siding on my house with gold trimmed soffit
Now one thing is left, what will I sell
I want a product so perfect it's like the ring of a bell
And that's when it hit me like one punch and two jabs
I would go into business selling pre-picked scabs
What will people do with them? Why should I care?
A scab sewed on to a leather jacket could be a really cool thing to wear
I'll package them in salt to keep their quality high
One scab might come from an elbow and another from a thigh
Well since I'll be in charge I'll have to find people to hire
And when it comes to creating scabs my employees will never have to retire
We'll suit them up in tank tops and shorts
and parade them down to the basketball courts
How about a rough game of basketball I manage to blab
And then I give them the ball, sit back and wait for the scabs
One foul, two fouls, three fouls, four
As I watch the scabbing process begin, I sit and wait for more
Push him down! Trip her feet! I yell and scream from the bleachers
New possible employees start to gather to watch their clot forming, scab performing teachers
Show these onlookers how to push someone down I yell to Rob
With so many scabs forming he looks like a blob
Come and take a rest I yell, as he limps in with a bloodied shin
But secretly in delight I can't wait for the scabbing process to begin
Alright that's enough I yell to the team
Now it was time to complete the second part of my scheme
Everyone go home and get a good rest
But whatever you do, don't bandage those wounds, and then a few of the tough guys beat their Chests
Tomorrow soon came and I was excited
My house was the meeting place and anyone with a scab was invited

I passed around bowls and felt such suspense
Our scab picking party was about to commence
Away they went, screaming and yelling
Newly picked scabs were what I would soon be selling
Filling up the bowls with scab upon scab
I felt like a scientist with guinea pigs in his lab
Here is your salary I waved to them in the air
One dollar bills, then I braided them in their hair
They were too bloody to handle this money
let's just say gettin' paid for your scabs can make you look pretty funny
Away they all left dripping blood on my floor
I looked at my bowls of scabs and I only wanted more
But then I realized, "No, on second thought, this is actually a great start.
After all, it's amazing how many scabs you can get when everyone does their part."
I packaged up the scabs and sent them to my marketing director
The public would be my investment and I would be the collector
Just as you might have thought the scabs were an instant hit
The only question now was how rich could I get
Scabs on shoes, scabs in cars, scabs for every meal
Now every time a scab was being picked someone was cutting a deal
Three years later after my company had reached the top
I sold it to an investor who believed this trend would never stop
I couldn't help but agree with him as I left my old office in a cab
What could possibly be more appealing than a freshly picked scab?
Now that I'm set for life and I have not a worry in the world
Now that I've married a beautiful wife with one boy and two girls

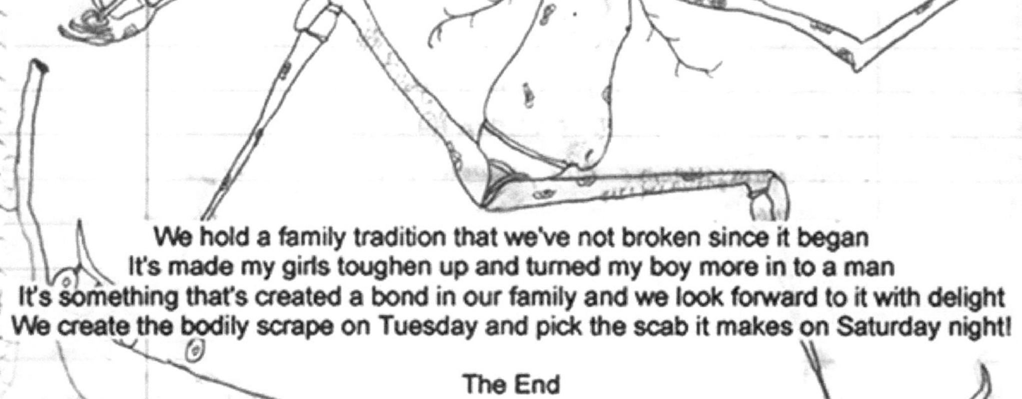

We hold a family tradition that we've not broken since it began
It's made my girls toughen up and turned my boy more in to a man
It's something that's created a bond in our family and we look forward to it with delight
We create the bodily scrape on Tuesday and pick the scab it makes on Saturday night!

The End

Jee Fu Nat
SUPER BURGERS
PEPSI
Dr Pepper
FUTURE
FU NATIONAL COMPETITION

Jee Fu National Competitions represent an emerging cutting-edge sport that is defining a new generation of MMA as it infiltrates tv networks across the Nation. Combining a bold selection of Olympic floor equipment with a "grab bag" of violent elements from traditional cage fighting, & yet still managing to mix in the global artistry of competitive salsa tap dancing, challengers receive scores from judges as they execute as many bizarre stunts as possible trying to knock out their opponent within the allotted time, all while performing choreography to famous salsa tunes which are remixed to dub step by a house DJ.

Don't mess with the Zen Master

The Problem with Nomads

"Once lived a Nomad." Claimed Denny Skaggs
His mouth spitting saliva, his lips like two wet rags
A story he'd told a million times
Mostly to his local community, in a small town called "Grimes"
The townsfolk were stragglers and travelers and such
If one wasn't Irish, you could bet he was Dutch
And oh rah ree how he called them by name
Off Donavitch, off Yactaw, he'd loudly proclaim
As they beckoned him further to complete his tale
Of the once lived Nomad and his southern wassail
And then Denny screamed in un-translated Egyptian
"why must you demand such detailed descriptions!?"
and from that day forward the people were brisk
the remainder of the tale held defiantly in Denny's clenched fists
he began to find other ways to take up his time
Researching things in the library like fungi and slime
He bought up some stock in a slushy called, Slorps
And analyzed the deterioration rate of a rotting rat corpse
His reputation altered as he had his fun
For the people now referred to him as the prodigal son
So Denny, so rare, so humbly denied
His hair dripping with oil, his lips crusted and dry
Decided to suddenly shout something in haste
His nostrils flaring as snot dripped down his face
"Twill I build me a ship with muck tar and glue
from the sweat off my back to the gum on my shoe."
And in a matter of minutes the masterpiece complete
A systematic luxury boat for the highly elite
"But it is only I who is worthy of taking a ride,
like a pair of fresh roller blades my wing tips will glide."
And glide he did in the whisp of the night,
Every emotion jolted as he was enflamed with fright
He did not know if the boat would indeed sail
And he no longer cared about Nomads who drank southern wassail
He landed in Graceland on the celebration of his birth,
Performing metaphysical rituals as he examined the earth
Eventually arriving to a threshold quite brickened
With armpits deodorized and greasy thighs slickened
Presents were waiting from family members abroad
Bestowing celebratory gifts, eating gizzards barely thawed
enjoying the reunion, as they lightheartedly gave each other greif
slamming their heads in to the walls and pulling out each others
teeth

Yet Denny still had a dream to wish on the cake
One of those rare moments when everything is at stake
And for dreamers like Denny who have traveled afar
With width and height resembling Kareem Abdul Jabbar
It wouldn't take a rocket scientist to guess what he'd do next;
Bite off the head of an earthworm, and rub turpentine on his neck

The End

1

Ain't Nobody Layin' a finger on my

Garden Buddy!

GARDEN BUDDY

2

Come'on George, you've <u>got</u> to tell me what you're hiding behind your back

I don't have to do anything...

GARDEN BUDDY

3

George... don't make me become someone I don't want to be...

oh my gosh dude, you need a breath mint, like, so bad.

GARDEN BUDDY

4

Dude, why are you acting like this? You're being such a dork-just let me see it, man...

Oh whoa, I didn't realize we both weren't just kidding around. Eric, I am so excited about you, your life, & everything that is ahead for you. I was going to wait to give this to you, but next to my shoe there is a small box that my grand-papi gave to me before he died. In it, there is an unopened package of 20 breath mints. Please feel free to take one. Seriously, dude...like right now.

GARDEN BUDDY

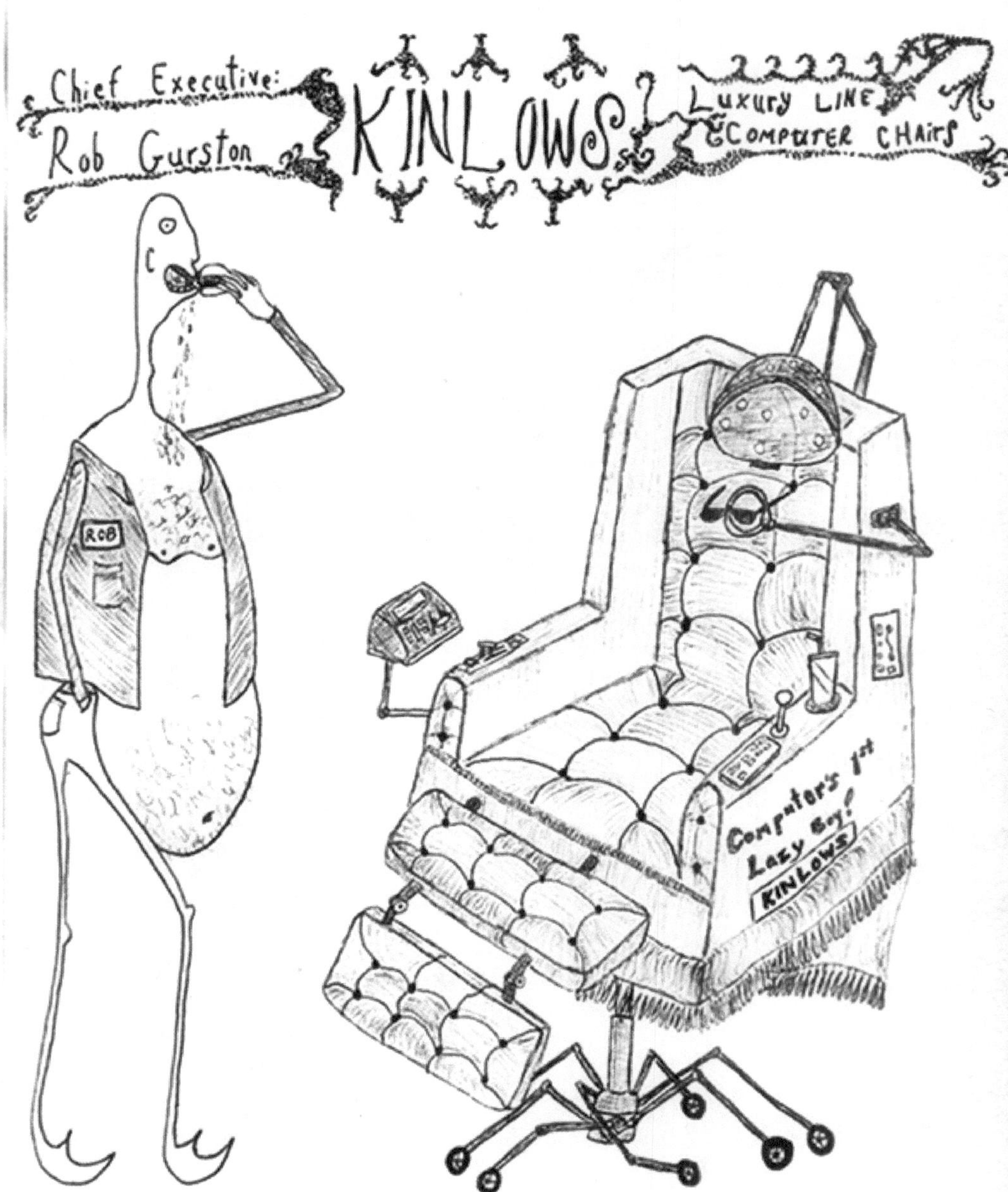
Chief Executive:
Rob Gurston
KINLOWS
Luxury LINE
& COMPUTER CHAIRS
ROB
Computer's 1st
Lazy Boy!
KINLOWS

What it Means to be Draped in a Doctoral Robe

My name is Rob Gurston and I like to blab
You start the foundation of the conversation and I'll pour the slab
Not Sure How it happened but one day I became a designer
Ended up making most of my money creating Kinlow's luxury recliners
But what I'll design next will inspire the masses
I will have the kool-aid and people will be bringing me their glasses
What is it you ask, that will be uttered in every ear lobe?
I'm quite confident you've guessed it - it is the doctoral robe
Largely misunderstood, and incredibly underestimated
I will turn this odd academic monument into something that is celebrated
Everything else is so boring when compared with this scholastic treasure
A professional grade doctoral robe's worth simply cannot be measured
When it wears you - because of course you never wear it
It should be tight around the neck and lose in the pits
It should drape you in luxury and flow freely as you walk
It should hover so indiscreetly as you murmur and talk
Worn properly, the robe's wide seems give your body a brand new depiction
Fully draped, it should allow arms and legs to move without restriction
But consider tying yourself to some cinderblocks if it is a windy city night
Because if you're not careful, you can become a doctoral robe kite
Whipped up in to the air and soaring across town
You will feel like a seagull as you fly all around
Wearing your doctoral robe to a dinner party will create lots of attention
Especially when you show off your doctoral robe modifier cycling system...one of my new inventions
The doctoral robe modifier cycling system is something special indeed
It allows you to move around in extra large robes, powered by the knees
It's basically a weird bike, with lots of positioner arms that are extended
You could try wearing the Quintuplet-X size robe without this special bike, but it's not recommended
The bigger the robe the better, that's what I always say
And thanks to the doctoral robe modifier cycling system, you can wear one every day
Another thing that's great about doctoral robes is that they're very discreet
Wearing one really comes in handy when I'm having a lot to eat
You see I'm kind of a messy eater and food tends to trickle down my chin
I just pull out the wide collar of my doctoral robe and those left over bites slip right in
I never thought a doctoral robe could hide so much half eaten food
Concealing a whole other meal spread across my collarbone that is just waiting to be chewed
Well I think you get the idea, Doctoral Robes are just plain great
They're the type of thing that anyone can look good in, even people who are really overweight
"One size fits all!" I proclaim to all mankind alike
As I ride around on my fully extended doctoral robe modifier cycling system bike

The bigger the robe, the better!!! and thanks to the Doctoral Robe Modifier Cycling System, sporting around the new Quintuplet-X size Doctoral Robe is as easy as, well...riding a bike!!!! Learn more on page 15...

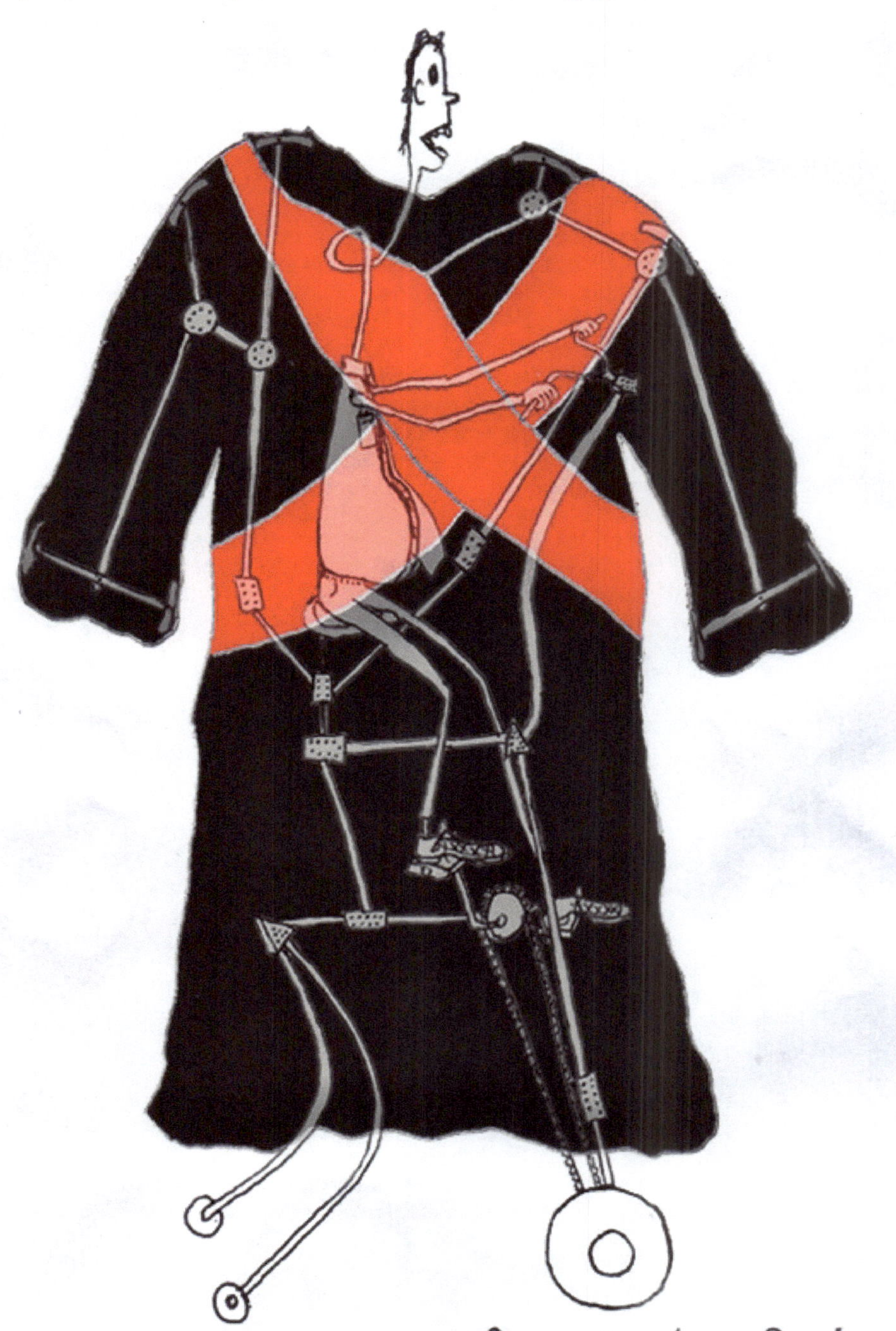

The Doctoral Robe Modifier Cycling System

Using break through technology, the new Doctoral Robe Modifier Cycling System works with the new Quintuplet-X size Doctoral Robes to create a seamless fit. The cycle's adjustable positioner arms allow you to "balloon up", taking full advantage of all the square footage the Quintuplet-X size robes have to offer. Order the Doctoral Robe Modifier Cycling System and start cycling around in your own Quintuplet-X size robe today!

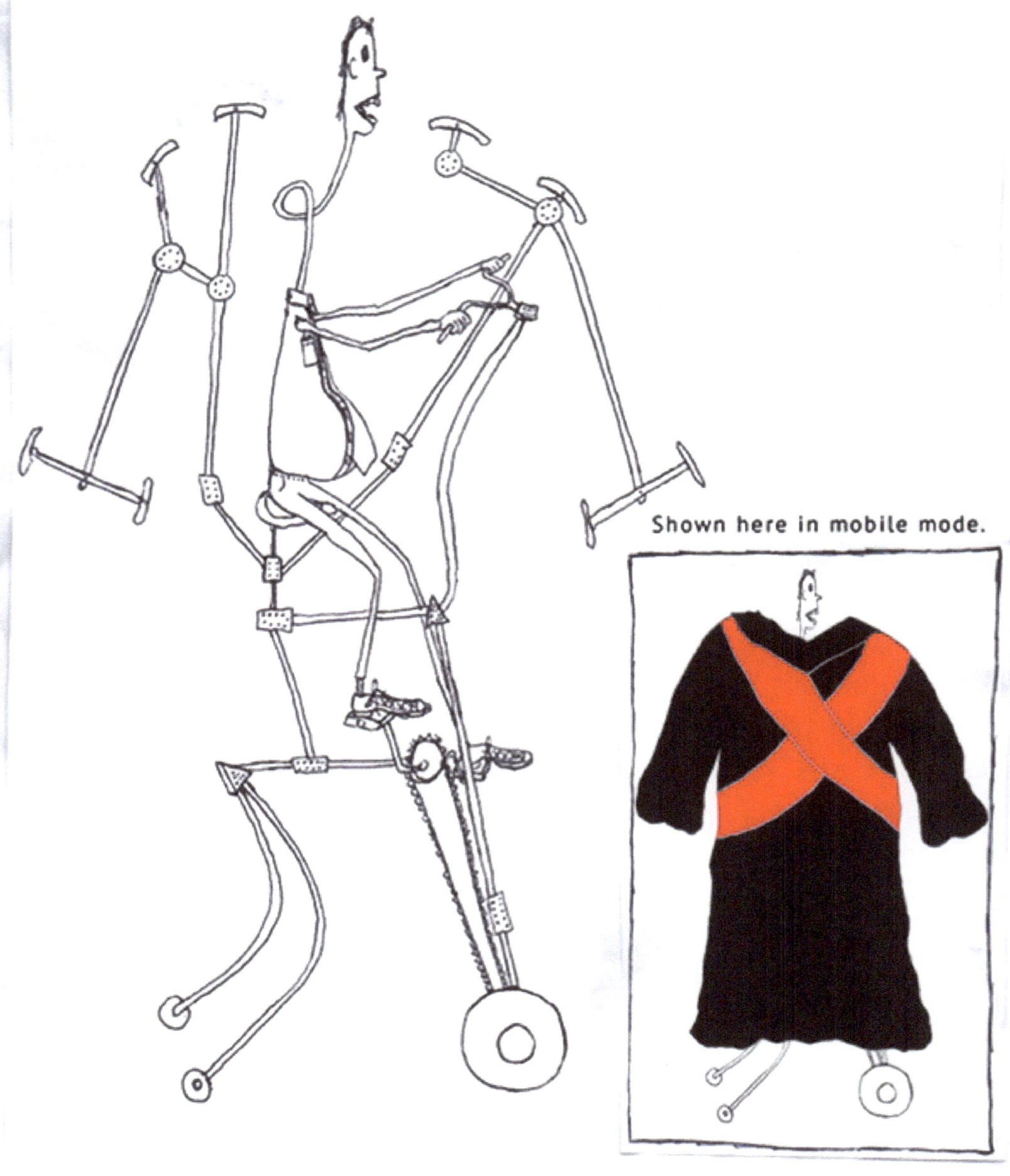

Shown here in mobile mode.

The Doctoral Robe Modifier Cycling System

Learning about frogs is hard work ...unless you have a plan.

Peering up at a ceiling that likely had the most popcorn texture ever sprayed on to any ceiling ever, Randy Witler realized he was awaking with only one eye open.

"Whoa," Randy said totally intrigued. He began practicing opening and shutting one eye at a time and after an hour had passed, Randy had "graduated" to a number of challenging eye tricks that, to his knowledge, had never before been attempted.

"I never knew I could do this," Randy said with more gurgle in his voice than I could possibly explain.

"If I get really good at this, I'll consider having a trophy made for myself every time I accomplish a new eye trick." And with that Randy decided to get out of his bed.

"Ooooohh!" yelped Randy.

He had forgotten about a 2 ft iron cast statue of a fund manager holding a hollowed out rake up to this lips and playing it like a clarinet that happened to be right by his bed. Randy had forgotten it was there and banged his right shin on the fund manager's "shoulder".

"I know that's gonna leave a bruise, I *know* it will." said Randy slipping into his morning snake skin slippers. As Randy breezed over to his kitchen area, he let his mind race with possible breakfast ideas. Eggs over easy, toast with jelly, wheat grass supplement drink, bacon and ham... Then Randy suddenly put on the brakes.

"Bacon and ham! Now that's definitely something that's gonna be do-able!" Randy yelled like a professional wrestler. Randy got that gig going on the stove and took a seat at his kitchen table. While he waited for the stove to warm up, Randy grabbed a hammer and some nails and practiced his hammering skills, meticulously whacking the nails into the table until they formed the spelling of his initials: R.W.

"Randy Witler ya'll, that's what I'm talkin' bout." Scurrying back over to the stove to make sure the meat was in the "sizzling" stage Randy added.

"They don't call me the "Sizzler" for nothing,"

As he sat there enjoying his piping hot breakfast trying not to burn his mouth with each bite, he stared out his kitchen window and watched a bird fly to a nearby tree branch, perch, then immediately fly away.

"Why do birds always do that? I mean they *always* do that," said Randy. He then noticed three things: a squirrel climbing down a tree, a spider making a web and that there was this really disgusting looking smudge on one if his windows. Transitioning his attention skyward, he soaked in the site of some interesting cloud formations. It was one of those mentally charged out of body experiences that made Randy feel like he was in the twilight zone. Then, all of a sudden, he noticed something pass by the window from top to bottom – almost as if it had fallen or been dropped.

"What the crust was that!? Randy belted in total shock. Even though the bacon and ham was tasty as all get-out, he couldn't deny what he saw. He had to go check it out. Once outside, Randy just about blew a vocal chord.

"I never would have expected this!" Randy said in a deep throat voice so powerful, it would probably put most hardcore metal band singers to shame. Right outside his door, sitting on a crispy dried leaf was a small frog leaning on it's side breathing hard. Randy quickly determined that this is what he must have seen fly by his window. It was clear the frog had misjudged a jump from the roof, sending it hurling to a life threatening impact near Randy's front porch. Realizing the next critical moments would determine whether the frog would pull through and make it, or give up and die, Randy remembered that in every dramatic war movie he had ever watched, the person who was dying always received a gut wrenching tongue lashing about how "they can't die...not now." Randy decided right then and there that if it could work in the movies, it could work for this frog. Tuning up his deepest deep throat voice, Randy prepared to give the frog a similar verbal assault in an attempt to save it's life.

"Okay little buddy, I bet here's what happened!" Randy screamed like a mad man.

"I bet you were sitting on the top of my roof and you decided that you wanted to go somewhere else, so you jumped! But you didn't realize how high up you were, so you basically ended up skydiving! I'm really confident that's what happened and I don't want to hear about any other conclusive possibilities – even if I'm wrong! (Randy made sure to include some reverse psychology statements designed to help the victim snap out of it) I'd rather believe a lie than hear you yap about what you think cuz let me tell ya something, I'm making the decisions around here right now and I say you're gonna live! So get off your side, sit up like a normal frog and deal with it!!!"

You could have cut the tension with a knife, but sure enough, straight out of a movie, the frog slowly pushed itself upright making a full recovery.

Randy was in shock. It had worked. Keeping the movie theme going, Randy proceeded to act out the typical heart wrenching ending of a film that features a human/animal friendship that is destined to come to an end against the will of both the animal and the human.

"Now I'm gonna make you hop around a little bit to make sure you're okay. What I'm about to do is for your own good."

Randy put his foot near the frog so that it would feel like it had to get away. It was effective. The frog jumped to a new spot and after Randy let out a breath of relief, he continued in character with an academy award winning performance.

"Now go on! Get outa here!" yelled Randy trying to muster up some tears. The frog didn't move.

"Didn't ya hear what I said little buddy!? You can't stay here. You're not welcome here anymore!!!"

Randy started throwing some nearby acorns which caused the frog to hop a few more times. Positioned half way between Randy's yard and the forest in back, Randy knew he had to pull out the classic family movie one liners used on animals that want to stay with the human, but need to leave for their own good.

"Don't you get it!? I don't *want* you anymore!! I *hate* you!! get out of my life! Go on, get!!!" Randy screamed throwing a huge handful of acorns at the frog. That did it. The frog jumped all the way in to the forest. Once the frog was out of sight, Randy went back inside to finish his bacon and ham breakfast. He was emotionally exhausted. Although he had just saved a frogs life by delivering the acting performance of his life, and although he should be experiencing total bliss because of it, the whole thing had left him with so many unanswered questions.

"I wonder what in the world that frog was thinking? That jump couldn't have been more irrational. Maybe it's just that I don't know anything about frogs..."

As Randy heard himself say that last sentence, it pierced him like a double-edged sword.

"Come to think of it, the only thing I know about frogs is how to get them to hop. That's easy, you just throw acorns at them."

Randy was starting to realize that when it came to frogs he was, for lack of a better word, clueless.

"There's just no excuse for not knowing anything about frogs. I mean if I knew *something* about them that would be different. But I know nothing about them and that just doesn't work for me. I've got to do something about this."

Randy knew he couldn't deal with this alone. He decided to say a prayer asking God to help him.

"Dear God, I'm in a mess. I know almost nothing about frogs. But I want to change that. I'm gonna work hard to learn about frogs and I know it's not gonna be easy. There's gonna be times when I feel like I don't care about frogs at all. I'm gonna get distracted, there might even be times when I want to quit. But I pray that you will give me strength to persevere. Amen."

Randy sat there a minute after finishing his prayer, then opened his eyes and said, "Encyclopedia Britannica, meet your worst nightmare!"

Randy spent the next few days trying to "figure this whole frog thing out." He called the zoo and talked to the "frog exhibit lady." He went to the library and checked out a bunch of books. They were actually from the kid section but don't think less of Randy for it. Randy actually had a pretty good reason for checking them out of the kid section. After spending time in the grown up section and reviewing a lot of the case study material, Randy noticed that the authors were "wrapping in" a lot of personal bias into the facts about frogs – "their opinions," "their views," "their ideas." Randy didn't want a hypersensitive view of frogs, he wanted the facts and he realized the kid section understood that. In the kid books, there weren't any emotionally influenced theories that muddied the simple truth about frogs. There was just information presented in an easy to read format. Randy loaded up.

With so much to learn about frogs, Randy didn't know where to begin and it wasn't until about the third day of gathering information that Randy came up with what he felt was a "strategy."

"Alright, I admit it, there's a heck of a lot to learn about frogs but with *this*...I'll be unstoppable."

Randy placed a sheet of paper in front of him showcasing intersecting lines that formed a one-month calendar.

"Introducing...my secret weapon." Randy proclaimed.

What Randy proceeded to do next was an act of sheer genius. Over the next three hours, referring back to the notes he had taken from the zoo helper, the internet, and the books he had checked out at the library, Randy created a month long lesson plan that explored twenty different fact based subtopics about frogs – and this is what it looked like...

Lesson Plan		**Unit Topic: Frogs**			
	Monday	Tuesday	Wednesday	Thursday	Friday
Week 1	Create a frog collage	Complete Pond shaped puzzle	Frog's Bag o' Bugs Activity	Analyze Lilly pads	Collect tadpoles
Week 2	Make frog noises for an hour	Life cycle of a frog Quiz	Free day	Find frog roadkill & dissect it	Color an entire "frog" coloring book
Week 3	Collect and Study insect "food".	Make frog mask	Conduct an interview with a frog "expert".	Eat fried frog legs	Free day
Week 4	Drink pond water	Complete Froggie facts Quiz	"Musical frogs": bonus challenge	visit frog museum	Leap frog Wrap up

"Armed with an outline like this, I feel completely confident that I will have mastered at least fourteen of the twenty subtopics presented in my lesson plan infrastructure and that makes me feel pretty cool."

Randy wasn't worried about whether he'd learn about frogs anymore – he *knew* he would. He had created a system. A system of success, and if he simply completed one lesson plan a day, just like the chart outlined, an increase in his knowledge about frogs would be practically guaranteed.

"I can't wait until my first lesson. I'm gonna do such a great job."

Randy was getting ready to embark on a whole new adventure and even though it would take some time, he felt like there was a great reward waiting for him at the end: the reward of a heightened sense of awareness about frogs.

Deciding to begin his first chart lesson the following Monday, Randy couldn't think of a better way to get psyched up for it than to play "Frogger" on Atari for thirty-six hours straight – and that's exactly what he did.

The End

THE ROMAN ELF

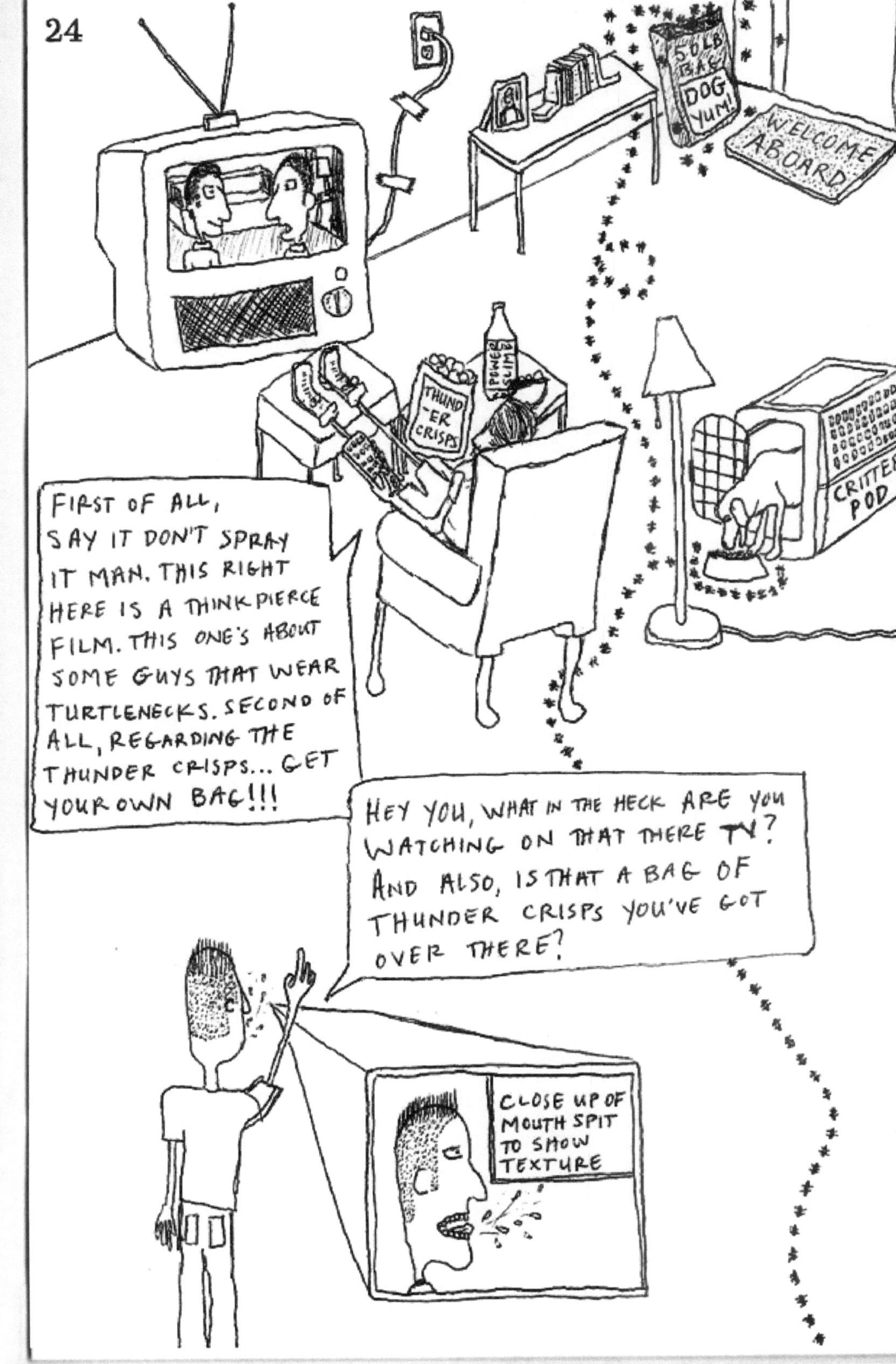
50 LB BAG
DOG YUM!
WELCOME ABOARD
THUND-ER CRISPS
POWER SLIM
CRITTER POD
HEY YOU, WHAT IN THE HECK ARE YOU WATCHING ON THAT THERE TV? AND ALSO, IS THAT A BAG OF THUNDER CRISPS YOU'VE GOT OVER THERE?
FIRST OF ALL, SAY IT DON'T SPRAY IT MAN. THIS RIGHT HERE IS A THINK PIERCE FILM. THIS ONE'S ABOUT SOME GUYS THAT WEAR TURTLENECKS. SECOND OF ALL, REGARDING THE THUNDER CRISPS... GET YOUR OWN BAG!!!
CLOSE UP OF MOUTH SPIT TO SHOW TEXTURE

THINKPIERCE 

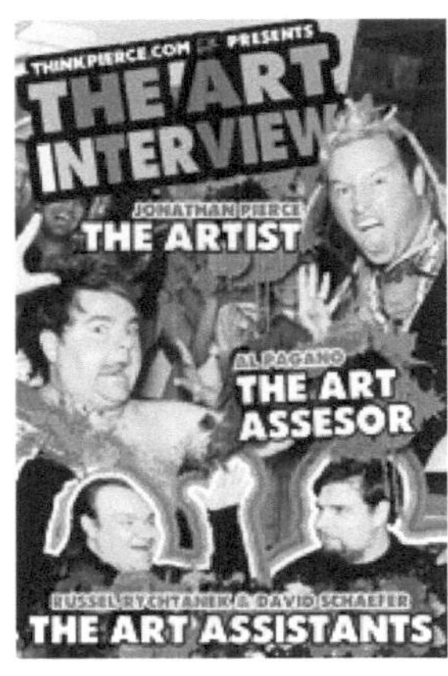

AVAILABLE AT

THINKPIERCE.COM

Barg arose quite early, on that special day
Then quickly inspected his back left molar which had been starting to decay
he fired up his hog; a supped up motorbike with attitude
the kind of bike that nick named him, "the big bad neighborhood dude"
But as he revved his hog on the street, he shed a pain filled tear
For one of Barg's toenails had just gotten ripped raw after getting wedged between a gear
To mask the pain he stopped at a local diner to fill his starving belly
By now the blood from his toe was crusting over like a blob of month old jelly
You would think it would gross people out, but just the opposite was taking place
They all wanted Barg's autograph, and photos of his bloodied toe near their face
The customers became obsessed with it, demanding the toe be put on display
Barg got so freaked out by the attention, he just wanted to get away
But it was too late for Barg, the word had already gotten out
The whole town wanted to see what this special toe was all about
Back to the road, Barg Bumbled like a Bee
His hog was taking him on a journey that would be impossible to foresee
Channel 9 was chasing him, right beside the girls
Journalists raced behind as well, hoping to share this story with the world
Then out of nowhere, the earth began to shake
Barg's motorbike was thundering, his nerves were wide awake
Suddenly he vanished; his chasers dropped their jaw
They then formed discussion groups, trying to make sense of what they saw
After hours of searching, they retired to their homes
Snacking on moldy raisin bran and recently expired Honeycomb
Then like a flash of lightening their t.v. screens flickered
Everyone tensely gripped their remote as they waited for the kicker

Then to everyones shock, Barg leaned in to the screen
he was a little nervous, but well dressed and quite clean
He motioned for the camera man to zoom down towards his feet
As he began to talk, everyone was on the edge of their seat
"Folks, as you can see, I've partially turned in to a slug
I needed some time to work through this, because I'm basically a bug
When I visited the clinic for my toe, they pulled my birth information
Turns out my mom was human, my dad was a rare sea creature, and I'm the result of the combination
My bloodied toe, triggered a scientific reaction
A "jabba the hut-like" substance replaced my legs in a metabolical transaction"
And as Barg explained to the people at home, nobody could deny
The slug-like torso that flowed down from his hips, where there used to be 2 thighs
But unlike you might think, what happened next took a surprisingly positive route
Barg's story touched the world that day, and they wanted to help him out
A local motorbike company came up with something unquestionably unique
They decided to create a motorbike that mimicked Barg's slug-like physique
The bike's front half sported a regular wheel & the back connected to a wad of slimy goop
The new motorbike actually gained popularity despite looking like a piece of poop
People learned to do cool tricks on it and it started gaining attention
Eventually becoming part of the x-games, showcasing it's one of a kind suspension
Then one day, accepting a special x-games award, Barg stood in front of a crowd
As he soaked in the site of the slug-like bikes he couldn't be more proud
And just as Barg was about to grab a corndog at the nearby concessions
A reporter caught him off guard by asking him the following question
"So Barg, who would you like to thank most for the success of these new slug-bikes?"
The crowd went wild as Barg just pointed back to his human mother to the left of him, and his sea creature father to his right

The End

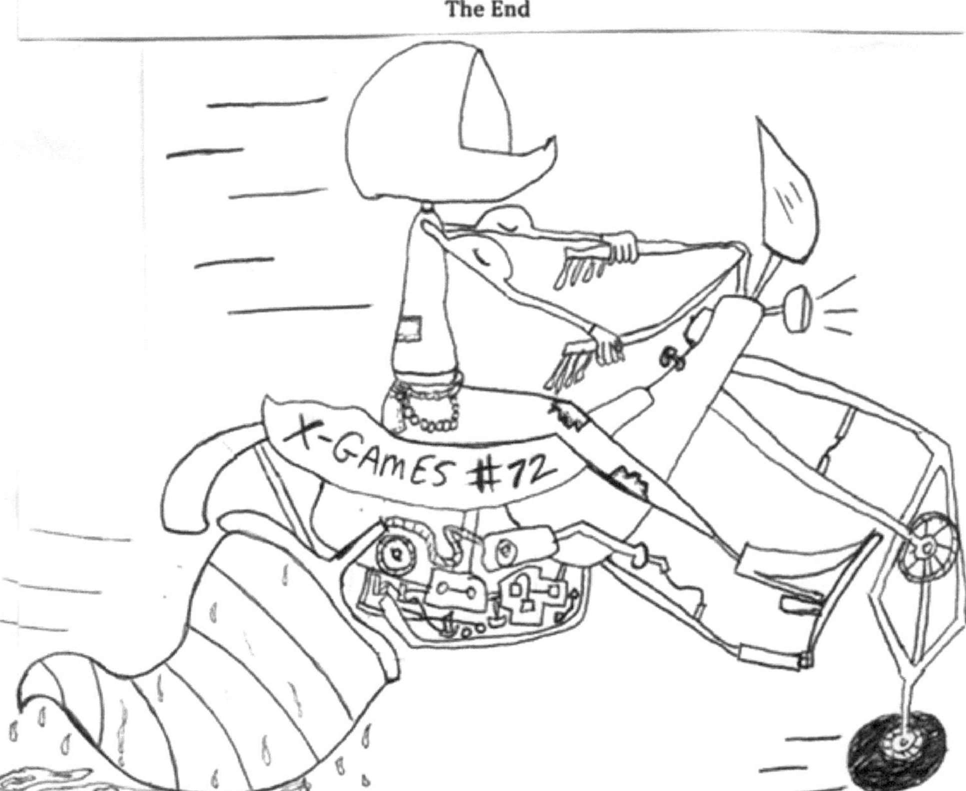

The End, Dude.

Examine more crust by
Jonathan at Thinkpierce.com

www.ingramcontent.com/pod-product-compliance
Lightning Source LLC
LaVergne TN
LVHW052303100826
845147LV00001B/125